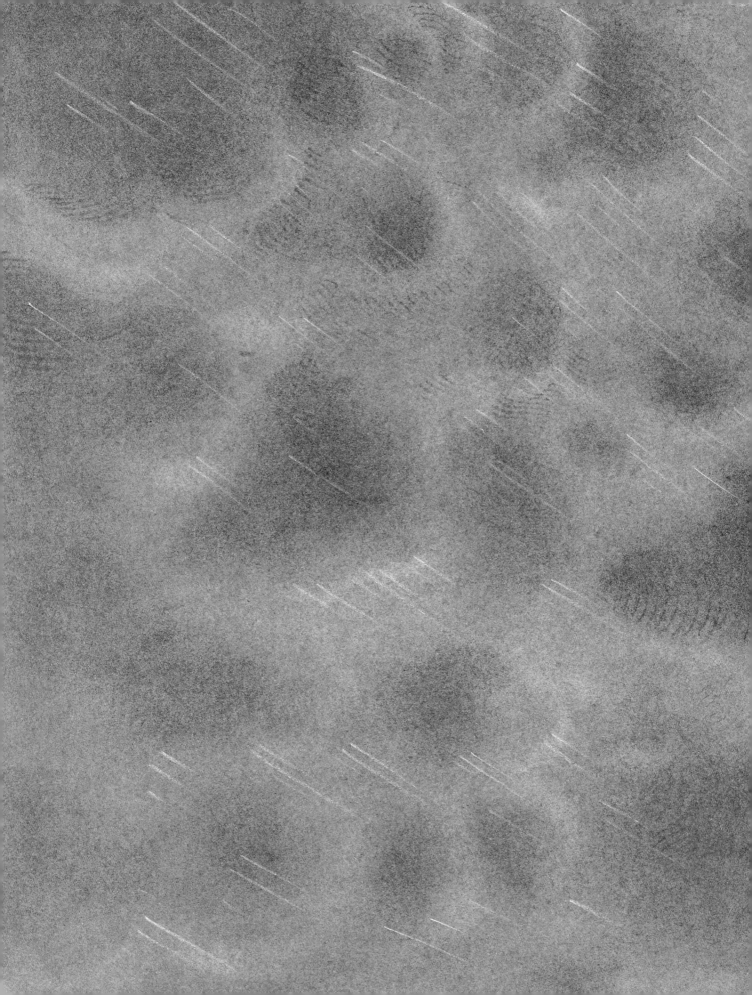

To Sam Alexander
A.B.
In memory of Douglas Brown
I.B.

A PICTURE CORGI BOOK: 0 552 54518X

First published in Great Britain by Doubleday,
a division of Transworld Publishers Ltd

PRINTING HISTORY
Doubleday edition published 1997
Picture Corgi edition published 1998

Picture Corgi Books are published by Transworld Publishers Ltd,
61-63 Uxbridge Road, Ealing, London W5 5SA,
in Australia by Transworld Publishers (Australia) Pty. Ltd,
15-25 Helles Avenue, Moorebank, NSW 2170,
and in New Zealand by Transworld Publishers (NZ) Ltd,
3 William Pickering Drive, Albany, Auckland.

Printed in Belgium by Proost

NOAH
~and the~
ARK

ANTONIA BARBER

Illustrated by
IAN BECK

PICTURE CORGI BOOKS

God made all things:
set the bright sun in the sky;
hung the pale moon in the heavens;
parted the day and night:
shaped the round ball of the earth,
blue with water, green with life,
set it among the stars:
made Man its master
to care for all creatures,
then turned away, pleased with his work,
and slept a while.

When God woke up, Earth had grown grey,
Man had grown mean.
Creatures cried out against his cruelty,
told God, 'This Man you made was a mistake!'
God sat and thought,
sorrowed and sighed,
said, 'I will wash clean this world
with a great flood,
and start again.'

But what of elephant with her enormous ears,
her incredible trunk?
What of magical-striped zebra,
leopard with his unchangeable spots,
head-in-the-clouds giraffe,
belly-on-the-ground snake
and all the rest?
Each one a masterpiece!
'Too good to waste!' thought God.
'Someone must save them...'

Noah was tending his farm,
doing no harm,
minding his own business...
when God chose him.
The voice came out of the clouds,
told Noah, 'Build Me an Ark.'
Noah, after the first astonishment,
asked God for guidance,
never having seen an Ark.

God said, 'Cut ribs of cypress;
cover it with reeds,
coat it with pitch.
Make it VERY BIG...
and order A LOT OF FOOD!'

Noah and his wife had three sons.
Shem and Ham shaped the ribs,
Japhet cut the reeds,
while Noah told everyone what to do;
as for their wives,
they did all the painting,
which was the best bit.

While they were building the Ark,
God spoke to the animals.
(They were less surprised,
being used to his voice.)
Each one turned at the whispered word.
They left plain and mountain,
jungle and desert,
burrow and tree-top
and set out on the long trail
to find the Ark.

Noah was loading when they arrived,
storing enough food for the long voyage.
When he saw the animals coming over the hill,
he doubled the orders!

The animals went in two by two.

When they were all inside,
God closed the door.

Then it began to rain.
Rivers began to rise,
slowly at first and then faster.
Soon they became torrents:
they broke their banks;
they drowned the fields;
they poured into the towns;
nothing could stop them.

The Ark began to float;
it was carried away by the flood.
At first it was very rough,
then very calm.
Even the mountain tops had vanished
beneath the waves.
Only the Ark remained.

For forty days it rained,
and for forty nights.

Inside the Ark it grew hot
and very stuffy.
The animals grew bored;
the animals grew restless.
Some of them mucked about.

The rain stopped at last
but the flood remained.
The Ark moved over the vast waste of water,
blown by winds, rocked by storms,
becalmed under a scorching sun.
The year turned;
the seasons passed over the earth:
spring without blossom,
summer without shade,
autumn without fruit.
While deep below the old world dissolved;
the sad cities crumbled and fell.
Washed by the clean salt waters,
the wounds healed, the scars faded
and the earth grew whole again.

One morning Noah opened the window;
the air smelt fresh and clean.
He sent out a raven to search for dry land.
All day they waited and hoped,
but the raven returned
tired and bedraggled.
When he opened the window again,
Noah thought he smelt trees.
He sent out a dove
which vanished into the blue distance.
All day they watched,
staring out over the endless water.
As night fell, they saw the dove returning
and, in her beak, she held a tiny leaf.

The news swept through the Ark:
the animals grew very excited.
No-one could sleep for the noise:
the roaring and trumpeting,
braying and chattering,
as they waited for the new dawn.
At first light, Noah set the dove free
and she did not return.

As swiftly as it had risen
the flood went down.
The Ark came to rest
halfway up a mountain.
It tilted to one side,
throwing everyone off balance.
Some of the larger animals trod
on some of the smaller ones,
so it took a while to sort things out.
At last, when they were all ready,
God opened the door.

W hen they saw the new world,
it left them breathless.
The sun was bright;
the air was clean.
Trees were springing up;
flowers were opening;
grass was spreading, thick and green,
across the plains.
Noah let down the ramp
and with a bit of pushing and shoving,
the animals went ashore.

Then Noah thanked God
for keeping them all safe from the flood;
and God thanked Noah
for looking after the animals.
'It was a pleasure,' said Noah politely,
'but please don't do it again...
the flood, I mean.'

'Never again!' said God
and his moving finger passed across the heavens,
leaving behind a bright rainbow
to sign his promise.

And to this day,
when storm clouds fill the sky
and the rain seems unending,
the rainbow comes,
sudden and magical,
and makes the dark world
new again.